J
904
MAJ

Major Disasters

CONTENTS

Flood Alert 2
Starving to Death 4
Hurricanes and Tornadoes 6
Slippery Slopes 8
Shaking Quakes 10
Violent Volcanoes 12
Deadly Diseases 14
Burning Issues 16
Tragedy on the Tracks 18
Watery Graves 20
Peril in the Sky 22
Crashing to Earth 24
Danger Below 26
Sticky Slicks 28
Nuclear Nightmares and
Chemical Catastrophes 30

Flood Alert

Swollen rivers, torrential rains, high tides, burst dams, thawing snow, hurricanes, earthquakes, and volcanoes can all cause flooding. Many people around the world live on low ground where they are at constant risk. Although we need water to live, our efforts to control it are often unsuccessful.

Bridge over troubled water
When the Mississippi burst its banks in 1927, 200 people climbed onto a bridge where they were stranded for three days without food before they could be rescued.

Most of Bangladesh is less than 30 ft. (9m) above sea level, putting it at risk from floods. In August 1988, 75 percent of the country was flooded and 3,000 people died.

Sinking cities

What do these cities have in common?
New Orleans
Caracas
Rio de Janeiro
Buenos Aires
Alexandria
Hangzhou
Rangoon
Karachi
Calcutta
Dacca
Cairo
Shanghai
By the end of the 21st century, they could all be submerged by tidal floodwaters.

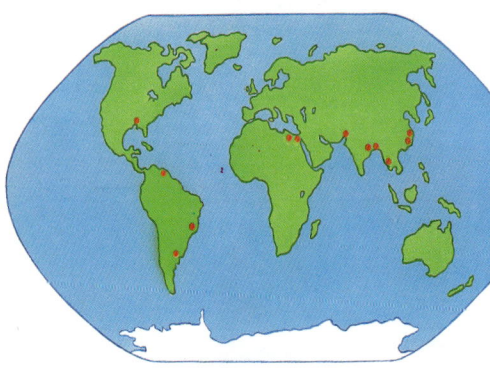

CITIES ON FLOOD ALERT

Noah's flood?
In the 1930s a group of archaeologists unearthed a 6 ft. (2m) layer of debris in Turkey. This was once part of the ancient kingdom of Mesopotamia. They believe that the silt was probably left by a huge flood that covered more than 40,900 square miles (102,400 sq. km). Some people think that this archaeological discovery proves that Noah's flood (described in the Bible) actually happened.

Record-breaker
In October 1887 the Huang He River (also called the Yellow River), in China, burst its banks, flooding 11 towns. More than 900,000 people drowned and a million more were made homeless.

Mighty wave
When Krakatau erupted in 1883 it caused tidal waves more than 120 ft. (36m) high—that's one-third of the height of the Statue of Liberty—to sweep across the coasts of Java and Sumatra, killing more than 36,000 people.

The monstrous molasses mess
In Boston, on January 15, 1919, a huge tank of molasses burst open and the molasses poured out onto the roads of the city. The massive brown blob gained speed and started to travel at 30 mph (48kmh)! The molasses tidal wave killed 21 people. Hundreds of volunteers were needed to clean up the sticky city.

Starving to Death

An absence of rainfall over a long period is known as a drought. If a drought affects an area or country where people depend on the rain for their crops, it can lead to famine and human tragedy on a massive scale.

Famines from history

Potato blight
In the 19th century the people of Ireland depended on the potato as the main part of their diet. But in 1845 and 1846 the crop was ruined by a disease called potato blight. One million people starved to death.

Midwest misery
During the 1930s in the U.S., severe drought hit farmland in the Midwest—turning it into a "dust bowl." Thousands of families faced starvation and were forced to leave their homes.

Pests

Entire harvests can be wiped out by pests, which swarm or scurry over crops, devouring everything as they go.

LOCUSTS

TERMITES

MICE

Starving to Death

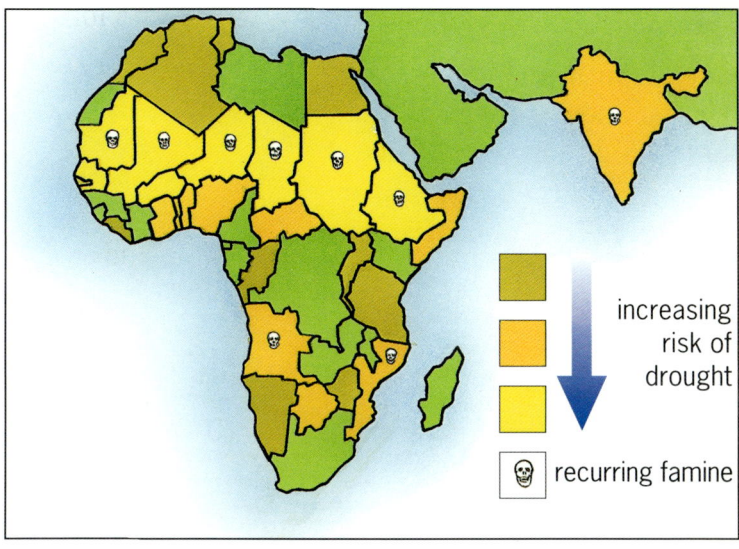

Regions of Africa and India have always been those hardest hit by drought and famine.

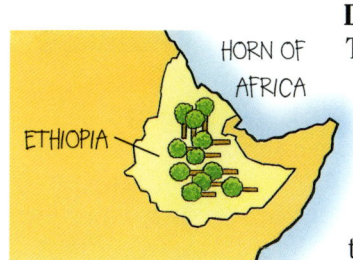

Disappearing forests
Trees once covered 30 percent of the land in the east African country of Ethiopia. Today only 3 percent of its land is forested, because trees have been cut down for firewood or to make way for farmland.

Too many people?
By the early part of the next century, the world's population could be double what it is today. Not only are more people being born, they also live longer. As we use up the earth's resources, how will we feed everybody?

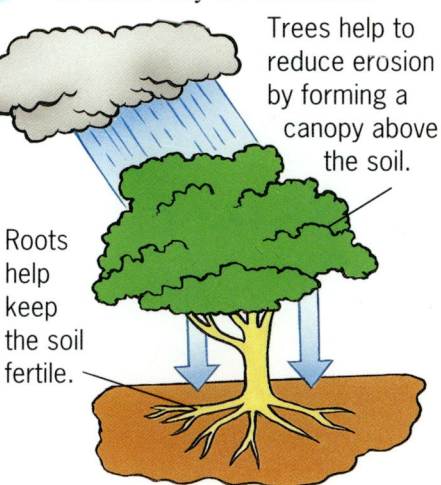

Trees help to reduce erosion by forming a canopy above the soil.

Roots help keep the soil fertile.

5

Hurricanes ...

Most of us have been in a storm at some time or another, but did you know that there are many kinds of storms? They move in different ways and at various speeds, look different, and cause varying amounts of destruction.

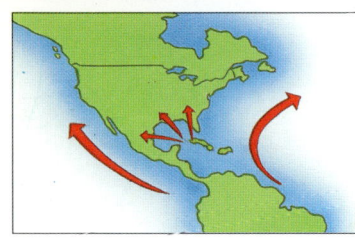

Hurricanes affect Caribbean islands and both the Pacific and Atlantic coasts of the U.S. People living in these areas are most at risk from hurricane damage between June and November.

Water storms
Hurricanes start at sea and move across the surface of the ocean, disturbing the water below. They can whip up 80 ft. (24m) waves that engulf ships and then smash into the land to destroy buildings and drown people.

What's in a name?
Each year hurricanes are given names starting with the letters of the alphabet in turn.

Counting the cost
The world's most expensive hurricane was Hurricane Andrew. It caused $22 billion worth of damage as it traveled across the Gulf of Mexico, Florida, and Texas in August 1992.

and Tornadoes

Tornadoes look like big curly storm fingers that spin overland at speeds of up to 60 mph (96kmh). They are smaller than hurricanes but are more powerful and can lift cars, trains, or even houses, into the air. The wind inside a tornado can spin around at 180 mph (288kmh).

Can you survive a tornado?
Many people have survived being sucked into tornadoes. Some have been tossed hundreds of feet into the air and carried several miles by these storms before miraculously being placed back onto the ground with barely a scratch.

Tornado Alley

An area of the central U.S. called Tornado Alley is struck by more than 700 tornadoes a year. On March 18, 1925, a tornado killed 695 people in three states.

Tornadoes are short-lived. They usually last less than an hour.

Slippery Slopes

When huge areas of snow or mud become unstable and begin to move downhill, the damage and death toll is devastating.

Peril in Peru

On May 31, 1970, an earthquake rumbled below Mount Huascarán in Peru. Snow on the mountain was loosened and a massive avalanche slid 10,000 ft. (3,000m) to engulf the villages below. It is thought that about 18,000 people were killed. The only people to survive were villagers who hid behind tombstones in the graveyard and were protected from the snow.

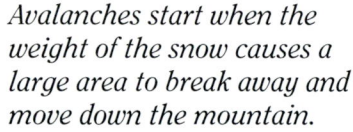

Avalanches start when the weight of the snow causes a large area to break away and move down the mountain.

8

Slippery Slopes

Rivers of mud
It isn't just great movements of snow that can cause disaster—a mud slide completely covered the town of Armero in Colombia in 1985, killing 21,000 people.

2. The volcano explodes.

3. Melted snow and mud move down the mountain.

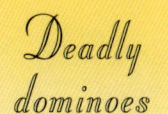

1. Gas builds up inside the volcano.

The volcano melts
People in the town of Armero did not think that they were in any danger. Although they lived next to a volcano, it had not erupted for 150 years. But in November 1985, the volcano exploded twice, melting the snow on its summit.

Stranded survivors
Some of the townspeople of Armero survived for up to four days after the disaster. But they eventually died, because the mud prevented rescue teams from reaching the victims in time.

> ### Deadly dominoes
> The worst landslide ever recorded hit China in 1920. A whole series of landslides was triggered off by an earthquake that rumbled in Kansu Province. The landslides followed one after another like a huge line of dominoes and killed an estimated 180,000 people.

Shaking Quakes

The surface of the earth is made up of plates that fit together like a giant jigsaw puzzle. These plates do not stay still but move infinitesimally across a boiling bed of molten lava. Sometimes the edges of the plates bang into each other. When this happens earthquakes rock the land above.

Over time the continents shift on the moving plates.

Concepción collapses
In 1960 the city of Concepción, in Chile, suffered the most powerful earthquake ever recorded. Nearly 6,000 people died. Elevated roads buckled like cardboard, sending vehicles falling to the ground below.

Shaking Quakes

Deep sea tremors
A monster wave 100 ft. (30m) high and traveling at hundreds of miles an hour hit Honshu in Japan in 1896, drowning 26,000 people. It was caused by an underwater earthquake that sent an explosion of water into the sky.

An earthquake in Mexico City in 1985 measured 8.1 on the Richter scale. Charles Richter invented this scale for measuring earthquakes. A seismometer picks up any tremors and draws them on a graph to show how violent they are (see below).

The worst earthquake?
In 1556 an earthquake tore apart the province of Shensi, in China, killing about 830,000 people.

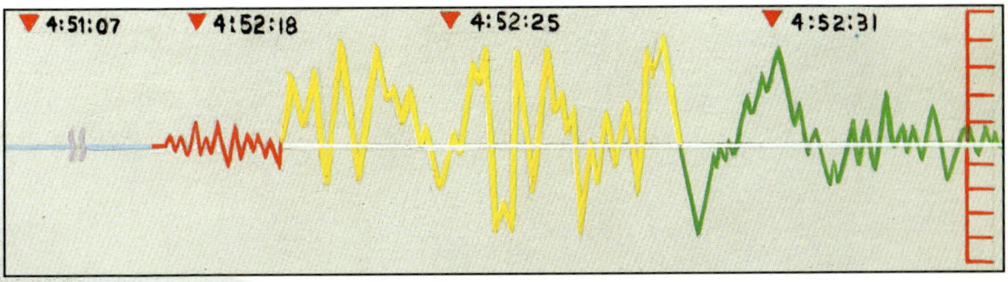

First seismometer

Each dragon's mouth on this Chinese urn held a small ball. If there was an earthquake, a ball would drop into a frog below to indicate which direction the tremors were coming from.

Violent Volcanoes

Volcanoes are spectacular fireworks displays that shoot gas and liquid rock into the sky. An erupting volcano can cover hundreds of square miles with debris and send suffocating gray ash floating halfway around the world.

Helen blows her top

1. In 1980 Mount St. Helens erupted. 2. The explosion blew a hole out of the side of the cone. 3. The height of the mountain was reduced by 1,280 ft. (384m). A vast new crater was created. Smoke from the volcano rose 20,000 ft. (6,000m) and ash was deposited 500 miles (800km) away. The blast flattened half a million trees over a radius of 15 miles (24km). Sixty people were killed by the eruption.

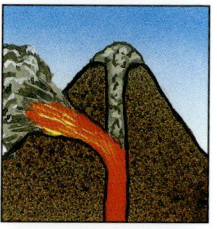

Molten lava flowing from Kilauea volcano in Hawaii in 1983.

Violent Volcanoes

The luckiest man in Martinique
In 1902 Mont Pelée in Martinique in the West Indies erupted. The only inhabitant of the town of St. Pierre to escape death was a prisoner in the town jail, who survived because the walls of his cell were so thick!

Roman remains
In A.D. 79 Mount Vesuvius erupted. It buried Pompeii in 20 ft. (6m) of volcanic ash and killed 2,000 people. When Pompeii was excavated, casts like this one were made by injecting plaster into holes in the ash that contained human remains.

Under the sea
Only about 1 percent of the world's volcanoes are on land. All the other volcanic leaks take place underneath the sea, where hot lava seeps up through gaps between the earth's plates.

Big bang
In 1883 the volcano of Krakatau, in Indonesia, erupted with such ferocity that it destroyed 163 villages. The noise of the eruption was so loud that it was heard across one-thirteenth of the earth.

Deadly burp!
In Cameroon in 1986 a volcano burped out a huge bubble of toxic gas and killed 1,700 people.

Pardon me!

Deadly Diseases

The biggest disease disaster of all time was the plague — also known as the Black Death. People caught the bubonic plague after being bitten by fleas carried by infected black rats.

Smoking was believed to protect the men who removed the bodies from catching the plague.

A horrible death
Plague victims developed large black sores followed by a severe fever. They coughed up blood and died after four or five days. The outbreak, from 1347 to 1351, wiped out almost a quarter of the worldwide population.

Quack quack!
Doctors of the day didn't know how to cure their patients. They wore masks with an herb-filled beak that they thought would stop them from catching the plague.

Deadly Diseases

Plague bombs
In the Middle Ages, soldiers used a particularly nasty kind of germ warfare. They catapulted plague victims over the walls of castles they were laying siege to in an attempt to infect the enemy.

Malicious malaria
More than 1 million people still die from malaria every year in the tropics. A person catches malaria when bitten by a female mosquito. Parasites carried by the mosquito enter the bloodstream and cause a fever.

Imported illness
In the 12th century, returning Crusaders brought leprosy to Europe from the Middle East. Lepers were forced to carry a bell and shout "Unclean!" to warn healthy people of their approach.

Tissue box
In 1918 a strain of the flu, called Spanish flu, started killing soldiers in the trenches of France. When World War I ended, the soldiers went home and took the virus with them. More than 21 million people died from the flu. Some people wore masks to protect themselves from the virus. Others used more bizarre methods of avoiding infection, such as covering themselves with bacon fat or sitting in ice-cold baths!

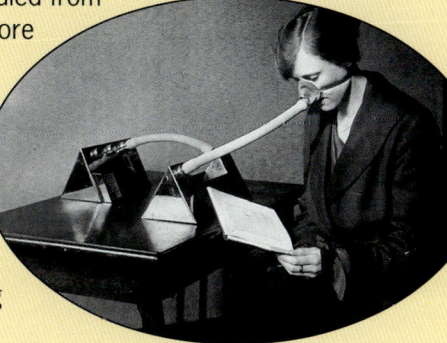

Burning Issues

Throughout history fires have given us warmth and cooked our food. But like water, fire can cause terrible destruction and loss of life if it is not controlled.

Flames in the forest
Forest fires can start from just one smoldering cigarette dropped by a careless tourist. Fanned by the wind, fire can devastate hundreds of square miles of trees.

Fire cones

The Monterey pine is unusual because its cones will release their seeds only if the tree has suffered fire damage. This is nature's way of making sure new trees will grow in an area that has been hit by a forest fire.

Burning Issues

London's great fire

On September 2, 1666, the Fire of London almost completely destroyed the world's largest city. It started in a street called Pudding Lane and spread quickly from house to house. In only three days 13,000 houses and 87 churches in 400 streets were destroyed. Amazingly, only eight people died, even though two-thirds of the city was burned to the ground. After the Great Fire, those who could afford it took out fire insurance. Firemen would put out a fire only if the house had a plaque to show it was insured.

A careless cow

The O'Leary family's cow knocked over an oil lamp while it was being milked and started a fire that tore through the city of Chicago on the night of October 8, 1871. The fire killed 250 people.

Nutty Nero

On July 19, A.D. 64, the mad emperor of the Roman Empire, Nero, ordered the city of Rome to be set alight. The fire ruined three of the city's 14 districts.

Tragedy on the Tracks

Ever since George Stephenson's *Rocket* killed a man on its first day of service in 1829 there have been rail disasters. Modern trains carry hundreds of passengers, and if something goes wrong, the scale of the tragedy can be horrendous.

STEPHENSON'S ROCKET

Death drop

More than 800 people died in a terrible rail disaster in Bihar, India, on June 6, 1981. The train's engine was pulling seven coaches across a bridge when the bridge gave way and five coaches plunged into the river.

Tragedy on the Tracks

BEFORE

...AND AFTER

Scotland's sorrow

In 1879 the Tay Bridge in Dundee was the longest in the world and a wonder of modern engineering. But on December 28 that year it collapsed. When a train from Edinburgh carrying 75 passengers failed to arrive in Dundee on time, the stationmaster crawled out onto the stricken bridge.

No survivors

Although a terrible storm was raging around him, the stationmaster could just make out that 13 of the bridge's 85 supports had gone—swept away by a huge gust of wind. He could see no sign of the train or of any survivors.

Worst wrecks

1981	Bihar, India	800 killed
1989	Chelyabinsk, Russia	up to 800 killed
1915	Guadalajara, Mexico	600 killed
1917	Modane, France	573 killed
1944	Balvano, Italy	521 killed

Watery Graves

The ancient Egyptians started to use the first sailing ships about 6,000 years ago. Over the centuries, sailors have set out on great voyages of discovery, but the history of seafaring has also had its share of tragedy and disaster.

The *Titanic* ... lost
The passenger liner *Titanic* was launched in 1912. She was 882.5 ft. (269m) long and weighed 47,069 tons. Her construction gave her the reputation of being unsinkable. Then, on April 14, the *Titanic* struck an iceberg. The order to abandon ship was given, but there were not enough lifeboats. Of the 2,200 people on board, only 700 escaped with their lives.

... and found
In 1986 Robert Ballard dived 2.5 miles (4km) to the seabed in a tiny submarine to explore the wreck of the *Titanic*.

Watery Graves

A Tudor tragedy
One of King Henry VIII of England's warships, the *Mary Rose*, was sent out in 1545 to face the French fleet. Just as the crew was hoisting her sails, she suddenly capsized. More than 600 sailors died.

MARY ROSE

Kublai Khan's fleet
Back in 1281, the Mongol emperor Kublai Khan tried to invade Japan for a second time. His entire fleet was destroyed in a violent storm, called by the Japanese, *kamikaze*, which means "divine wind."

Other disasters at sea
- The German liner, *Wilhelm Gustloff*, was sunk in 1945 by a Russian submarine with the loss of 7,700 passengers and crew. Only 903 survived.
- The 28th Fastnet race (off the west coast of Britain) was hit by atrocious weather. Of the 316 boats that started, only 128 finished, and 23 were abandoned or sunk.

Peril in the Sky

Statistically speaking, you're safer in the air than when you have your feet firmly on the ground. But when air disasters happen, they rarely leave any survivors.

Flying cigars
Before jumbo jets, airships were used to carry large numbers of passengers. They were like huge cigars made of canvas hung on a wooden or metal frame and were carried into the air by hydrogen gas.

Instant disaster
The Hindenburg airship exploded in New Jersey on May 6, 1937. Bystanders watched in horror as the 800 ft. (240m) craft burst into flames and burned to nothing in 32 seconds. Thirty-five people were either burned alive, or jumped from the ship and were killed by their fall.

All that was left of the Hindenburg after it exploded.

Peril in the Sky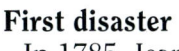

First disaster
In 1785, Jean Pilatre Rozier became the first person in history to die in an aviation accident. Rozier's huge silk balloon crashed into the English Channel only two years after he had made the first successful flight in this newly perfected invention.

PAN AM FLIGHT 103

Worst air disasters

583 people lost their lives in 1977 when two jumbo jets collided on the runway at Tenerife Airport.

520 people died in Japan in 1985 when their plane crashed into the side of Mount Ogura.

346 people were killed when a plane from Paris crashed just after takeoff in 1974.

Lockerbie
On December 21, 1988, Pan Am's flight 103 took off from London and headed for New York. Less than half an hour later a bomb went off in the luggage hold at the front of the plane. The aircraft lost power and dropped out of the sky like a stone. It crash-landed on the village of Lockerbie in Scotland, killing all 259 crew and passengers, and 11 people on the ground.

WRECKAGE OF FLIGHT 103

Crashing to Earth

Space has countless hazards. Earth has always been the target of bits of flying rock from outer space. Then, in 1961, the first astronaut was blasted into orbit and since then there have been 170 attempts to travel into space, each of them carrying with it the risk of disaster.

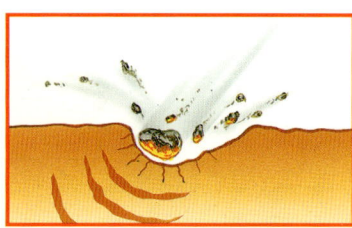

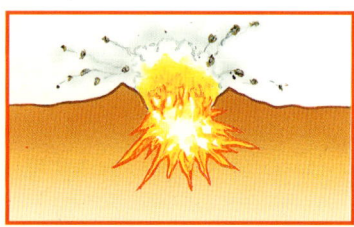

Space missiles
Meteoroids and asteroids are constantly hurtling toward Earth. These lumps of space rock usually burn up in the atmosphere, but some crash to the ground where the force of their impact makes huge craters.

The Barringer Crater in Arizona is 570 ft. (171m) deep and 4,150 ft. (1,245m) across. It is the biggest meteorite crater in the world.

Dino disaster
A massive asteroid fell to Earth about 65 million years ago. It sent huge clouds of dust into the atmosphere and set off earthquakes and tidal waves. Scientists think these dramatic changes may have caused the dinosaurs to die out.

Crashing to Earth

Challenger's crew of five men and two women.

Doomed mission
On January 28, 1986, the space shuttle *Challenger* took off from the Kennedy Space Center, Florida. After just 73 seconds into the flight, its left booster exploded, killing everyone on board.

In-flight fatalities

The first living thing to travel in space was a dog called Laika, in 1957. Poor Laika died when her oxygen supply ran out. After Laika, several other dogs and monkeys were sent into orbit.

The first human fatality struck in 1967 when the capsule of the *Soyuz 1* spacecraft crash-landed, killing the Russian cosmonaut on board.

25

Danger Below

Working or traveling underground can be extremely hazardous. When subterranean disaster strikes, there is nowhere for victims to run.

Terror on the subway

On November 18, 1987, 31 people died in London's King's Cross subway station when a fire started on one of its escalators.

BURNED OUT TICKET BARRIERS

Death blast

On October 14, 1913, the Universal coal mine in Senghenydd, Wales, exploded, causing the worst mining disaster Britain has ever known. A huge wall of fire blocked the entrance to the mine and cut off the miners' air supply. When firefighters finally got into the pit they managed to rescue 498 miners, but 400 were still trapped. Four days after the disaster the authorities had no choice but to seal the mine to prevent further explosions.

Danger Below

Early warning birds

Miners used to take canaries down into the pits with them. If the canary became drowsy or fell off its perch, the miners knew that there was a buildup of gas. As might be expected, this method of detecting gas leaks was not entirely foolproof. Canaries were also used in the trenches in World War I.

Exploding roads

Guadalajara in Mexico was shaken by 15 underground blasts on April 22, 1992. The explosions were caused by poisonous gases and gasoline combining in the sewers. The erupting gases threw cars into the air, ripped up roads, and destroyed buildings. More than 1,000 people were injured and 230 killed.

A woman leaving the rubble of her home in Guadalajara.

Tunnel tragedies

The Mont Cenis Tunnel was bored through the Alps between 1861 and 1870. In spite of safety measures, 28 workers died during the construction of the tunnel. Boring machines were replaced by blasting after 1875 and tunneling became more hazardous. The St. Gotthard Tunnel was completed in 1881, but at a cost of 311 lives.

Sticky Slicks

Oil is one of the world's most valuable natural products—that's why it's called black gold. Oil is transported across the world in supertankers, which can carry up to 250,000 tons. If the oil spills out it devastates the environment—damaging the land, poisoning the sea, and killing wildlife.

120,000 tons of oil spilled out from the Torrey Canyon *in 1967.*

Amoco Cadiz
Ten years after the *Torrey Canyon* spill, the *Amoco Cadiz* smashed onto some rocks off the French coast. The ship spewed out 250,000 tons of oil.

Eco-disaster
The world's first major oil spill took place in March 1967, when the *Torrey Canyon* was blown onto rocks off the coast of England. A hole 650 ft. (195m) long was torn in the ship's side. The oil poisoned British and French beaches.

Sticky Slicks

A Kuwaiti oil well on fire.

Waging war on nature
During the 1991 Gulf War, Iraqi troops set fire to 850 of Kuwait's oil wells. Oil escaped into the Persian Gulf damaging coral reefs, beaches, and mangrove swamps. More than 30,000 birds died from being smothered by thick crude oil.

The Exxon Valdez *disaster killed at least 980 otters and 33,100 birds.*

Alaskan leak
On March 24, 1989, the supertanker *Exxon Valdez* ran into rocks in Prince William Sound off the Alaskan coast.

A massive cost
It took 6,000 people and $643 million to clean up the *Exxon Valdez* spill—but the real damage caused to fishing businesses and destroyed breeding grounds can never be repaired.

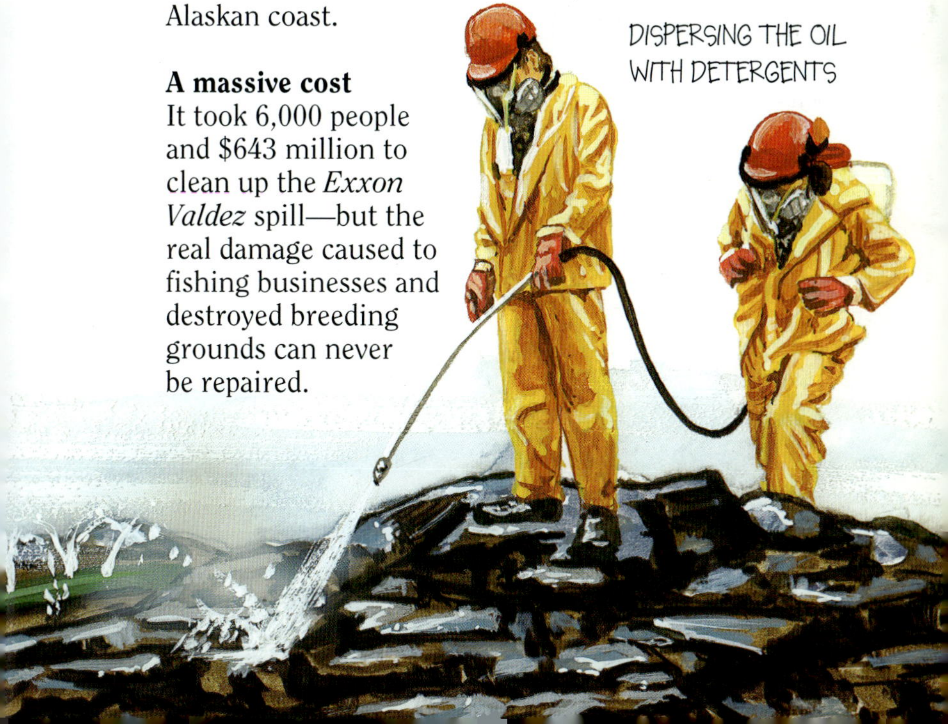

DISPERSING THE OIL WITH DETERGENTS

Nuclear Nightmares and

In 1945 the U.S. dropped the first atom bomb on Hiroshima in Japan, killing 80,000 people instantly. The same atomic energy is used today to generate electricity, but nuclear power plants can also explode, with devastating results.

Chernobyl explodes
Chernobyl's nuclear reactor exploded on April 26, 1986, when its radioactive core overheated. A massive cloud of deadly radiation was sent into the air.

Contaminated clouds
The radioactive cloud moved west, and within two days it reached Germany, Sweden, and Poland. Four days later the cloud was hanging over France and Britain, bringing with it radioactive rain. Soil, water, food, plants, and animals were all contaminated.

Map shows the radioactive cloud moving across Europe.

Chernobyl's legacy
The area around the Chernobyl power plant is still deserted—there are no trees and the cities are all empty. People can die of radiation poisoning years after being contaminated. Scientists think Chernobyl will claim 100,000 lives over the next 40 years.

Chemical Catastrophes

Bhopal—the killer factory
The Union Carbide chemical factory at Bhopal in India was built to make chemicals to kill the insects that destroy crops. But in 1984 it blew up, killing more than 3,350 people and injuring 50,000 others.

Poison blast
Just after midnight on December 3, the city of Bhopal was awakened by a huge explosion at the nearby chemical plant. A fog of poisonous chemicals leaked out and crept along the ground.

Human cost
All over the city people were choked by the chemicals and died in their sleep. Many survivors suffered hideous burns. More than 10 years later, people are still dying from the effects of the Bhopal explosion.

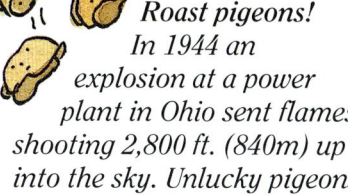

Roast pigeons! In 1944 an explosion at a power plant in Ohio sent flames shooting 2,800 ft. (840m) up into the sky. Unlucky pigeons flying overhead were roasted alive and fell to the ground.

Rush-hour horror
Ten people died and more than 5,000 were injured in the Tokyo subway when terrorists released canisters of the nerve gas sarin on March 20, 1995. Victims collapsed suffering from nausea. Sarin was first developed by the Nazis.